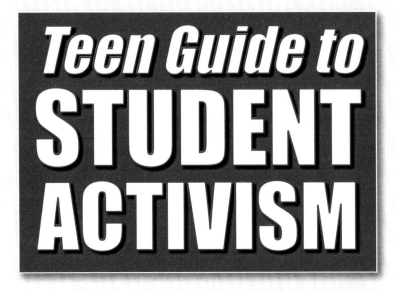

Teen Guide to STUDENT ACTIVISM

Stuart A. Kallen

ReferencePoint
Press®

San Diego, CA

ROCKFORD PUBLIC LIBRARY

ReferencePoint
Press®

About the Author

Stuart A. Kallen is the author of more than 350 nonfiction books for children and young adults. He has written on topics ranging from the theory of relativity to the art of electronic dance music. In addition, Kallen has written award-winning children's videos and television scripts. In his spare time he is a singer, songwriter, and guitarist in San Diego.

LIBRARY OF CONGRESS CATALOGING-IN-PUBLICATION DATA

Names: Kallen, Stuart A., 1955– author.
Title: Teen Guide to Student Activism/by Stuart A. Kallen.
Description: San Diego, CA: ReferencePoint Press, [2018] | Audience: Grade 9
  to 12. | Includes bibliographical references and index.
Identifiers: LCCN 2018031466 (print) | LCCN 2018043134 (ebook) | ISBN
  9781682825426 (eBook) | ISBN 9781682825419 (hardback)
Subjects: LCSH: Student movements—Juvenile literature. | Youth
  movements—Juvenile literature.
Classification: LCC LB3610 (ebook) | LCC LB3610.K35 2018 (print) | DDC
  371.8/1—dc23
LC record available at https://lccn.loc.gov/2018031466

CONTENTS

Creating Change

In February 2018 fourteen students and three staff members were killed by a gunman at the Marjory Stoneman Douglas (MSD) High School in Parkland, Florida. Seventeen others were wounded. Four days after the shooting, student activists at the school organized the March For Our Lives campaign (known by its Twitter hashtag #NeverAgain) to advocate for tighter gun control laws. Tens of thousands of supporters nationwide joined the campaign on social media in the days that followed. The movement culminated when an estimated half-million people participated in the March For Our Lives demonstration in Washington, DC, on March 24. Millions of others attended related rallies in eight hundred cities and towns around the world. Before the event one of the student leaders, seventeen-year-old MSD high school senior David Hogg exclaimed, "We're teenagers and we're leading a national movement."[1]

Student activists like those in the Never Again movement have made a commitment to get involved with causes that matter to them. The students are standing up, speaking out, and marching to bring about change. And in doing so, they are taking part in a revered American tradition. In the twentieth century young activists successfully campaigned against child labor, racial segregation, and the Vietnam War. In recent years student activists have taken leading roles in the March For Our Lives campaign, the United We Dream immigration protests, and the Black Lives Matter movement.

Leading and Learning

Large national movements like these attract a lot of attention. But not all activism takes place on a national stage. Most student activists work at the local level. They volunteer in many capacities—tackling local issues such as homelessness, lack of school funding, bullying, discrimination, sexual abuse, and more.

Olivia Kriegsman of Poway, California, took a homegrown approach to fixing a potential problem. She wanted to spread the message of healthy eating to other young people who might not have access to healthy foods. For her Girl Scout Silver Award project, in 2017 she developed a six-week program for elementary and middle school students living in a low-income housing community. Participants in the program learned about the importance of eating fruits and vegetables and other healthy foods. In 2018 Kriegsman's program earned an award from the Prudential Spirit of Community Awards program, which recognizes achievements in student volunteerism.

Sometimes young activists use what they have learned at the local level and put it to work to drive a national movement. Jenni Li, a Washington, DC–based activist, became politically active in high school after a teacher suggested she attend meetings by neighborhood student activists who focused their efforts on ending sexual harassment. Engaging in this type of activism was easy and satisfying, according to Li: "I just showed up. They always had a plan, so I could just follow along and be helpful."[2] Li went on to use her neighborhood experiences to organize numerous national social justice projects aimed at protesting sexual assault and racism.

The Social Media Amplifier

Whether the efforts of young activists are aimed at creating change at school, in a city, or across the nation, they use time-honored techniques to amplify their message. They recruit members, research issues, develop strategies, raise money, circulate petitions, speak to media outlets, lobby politicians, and publicize

Thousands of protesters, led by high school students and other young people, march through Columbia, South Carolina, on March 24, 2018, to demand common-sense gun laws. Similar student-led protests attracted thousands more marchers across the nation.

events. Modern activists are also adept at using Facebook, Twitter, Instagram, Tumblr, and other social media sites to organize and mobilize. These go-to organizing tools allow student activists to sign up volunteers, post articles, share videos, and provide information about upcoming meetings and events at an unprecedented speed. As student rights lawyer Frank LoMonte explains, "Social media has just been the great leveler. It turns days into hours and hours into minutes."[3]

Social media also allows activists in marginalized communities to find one another, attract supporters throughout the world, and organize around common issues. Activists who coordinate their activities on Twitter and other platforms can speak in an amplified voice that delivers a strong, unified message to the public and the media.

Developing Life Skills

Social media helps motivate students to support a cause when they might otherwise remain on the sidelines. Perhaps this is why so many students now claim to be activists. According to a 2017 report by the National Survey of Student Engagement, one in eight college freshmen self-identify as an activist. Activist actions they had taken include submitting demands to an administrator, participating in a protest, or helping organize a strike, boycott, or walkout. The report says the activists seem to have broader life skills than their nonactivist peers. They interacted more often than nonactivists with people of different racial and religious backgrounds, gender orientations, and political views. According to the report's authors, "Student activism appears to signal [an increase in] reflection, critical thinking, and engagement with ideas, combined with a vision for change."[4]

While making the world a better place, student activists develop valuable skills that last a lifetime. Student activists learn to speak in public, negotiate, educate, and persuade others to consider their point of view. They develop critical-thinking skills and devotion to their communities that can set the stage for a lifelong love of civic engagement. As Kriegsman says, "I learned . . . leadership and I expanded my skills, like thinking on my feet when things do not go as planned. I also learned to be grateful for what I have, because not all are as fortunate as I am."[5] When working for a favorite cause, student activists amplify their voices, drive the debate, and fight today for a better future tomorrow.

> "I learned . . . leadership and I expanded my skills, like thinking on my feet when things do not go as planned."[5]
>
> —Olivia Kriegsman, nutritional workshop organizer

CHAPTER 1

Can Students Make a Difference?

"If you just use the little bit of courage you have, to speak up for something you believe in, you'll be amazed at what a difference you can make. You don't have to be some great hero, some really great courageous person. . . . Just use the little bit of determination that you have."

—Mary Beth Tinker, thirteen-year-old antiwar activist

Quoted in American Civil Liberties Union of Tennessee, "Stand Up/Speak Up: A Guide for Youth Activists," 2015. www.aclu-tn.org.

At age eleven Marley Dias was already an avid reader, but she was frustrated by the book assignments at her West Orange, New Jersey, school. Her 2015 reading list required students to read classics like *Shiloh*, *Old Yeller*, *and Where the Red Fern Grows*—all stories about boys and their dogs. Dias appreciated these books, but as an African American girl, she was disappointed that her reading list did not include a single book with a black, female character. Dias jumped on her computer to look into this a bit further. What she discovered was that less than 10 percent of all children's books published in 2015 featured a main character who was black. She explains why this bothered her: "If there are no black girl books as part of the school curriculum, then how are we expected to believe all that stuff that teachers and parents are constantly telling us about how we're 'all equal'? . . . If black girls' stories are missing, then the implication is that they don't matter. I didn't like it so I had to do something."[6]

Although only in fifth grade, Dias came up with a plan. As a fan of online cat videos—which often attract millions of "likes"—Dias was aware of the power of social media. This led her to launch the #1000BlackGirlBooks campaign in November 2015. The goal was to inspire users of social media to donate one thousand copies of books that featured black female characters. She planned to give the books away to schools and libraries. As Dias puts it, "Soon everybody would be reading about awesome us."[7] Dias was too young to have social media accounts, but with her mother's help, the hashtag was posted to Facebook, Instagram, and Twitter.

Power in Numbers

Like many young activists, Dias knew that there is power in numbers. She understood that her chance for success would increase if she could recruit people to help make her idea reality. She needed help from other students who shared her passion, patience, persistence, and organizational skills. Dias quickly connected with around twenty girls at her school; they call themselves the Super-Girls Society, or SGS. One SGS member, Amina Anekwe, was a math honors student who had worked on a campaign to get more girls interested in math and science. Anekwe tried to make these subjects fun by creating games and hosting a math tournament with a disc jockey and dancing. Another member of the SGS, Tori Fergus, had created a program called Room for Change to decorate rooms for homeless teens who stay at the Newark, New Jersey, YMCA. Fergus convinced IKEA and Home Depot to donate bath and body products, furniture, and other products so that the teens could feel compassion from the local community even though they were experiencing tough times. The SGS did more than bring experience to the cause, as Dias explains: "Working with friends who are committed to social justice and doing good can help make activism fun, even though it is also challenging. Activism is hard and fun."[8]

> "Working with friends who are committed to social justice and doing good can help make activism fun, even though it is also challenging."[8]
>
> —Marley Dias, founder of the #1000BlackGirlBooks campaign

The #1000BlackGirlBooks hashtag went viral, and within four months Dias had collected more than four thousand books. The campaign attracted the attention of mainstream media personalities. Dias was asked to appear on *The Ellen DeGeneres Show*, where the host gave her a $10,000 donation. Dias even obtained a book deal of her own; her memoir, *Marley Dias Gets It Done: And So Can You!*, was published in 2018. As Dias explained, she wrote the book "so other kids can learn how they can use their gifts, talents and passions to make a change in the world. I also wanted adults to know what they could do to help kids change the world."[9] The book provides how-to information for student activists, with a strong focus on ways students can use online platforms to advance the causes they believe in.

When Dias launched #1000BlackGirlBooks, she thought one thousand seemed like a suitably large number to set as a goal. But the campaign far exceeded her expectations. By 2018 Dias

Eleven-year-old Marley Dias (pictured) was frustrated by the absence of books with black, female characters on her school reading list. She launched a social media campaign to get more diverse books into schools and libraries.

Start a Campaign

When eleven-year-old Marley Dias launched the #1000BlackGirlBooks in 2015, she was frustrated that her school's reading list did not feature a single book with a black, female character. In 2017 Dias told *Forbes* that she had three options about how she might address the problem (she went with option 3):

> Option 1: focus on me, get myself more books; have my dad take me to Barnes and Noble [bookstore] and just be done, live my perfect life in suburban New Jersey. Option 2: find some authors, beg them to write more black girl books so I'd have some of my own, special editions, treat myself a bit. Or, option 3: start a campaign that collects books with black girls as the main characters, donate them to communities, develop a resource guide to find those books, talk to educators and legislators about how to increase the pipeline of diverse books, and lastly, write my own book, so that I can see black girl books collected and I can see my story reflected in the books I have to read.

Quoted in Maggie McGrath, "From Activist to Author: How 12-Year-Old Marley Dias Is Changing the Face of Children's Literature," *Forbes*, June 13, 2017. www.forbes.com.

was planning to collect and distribute 1 million books featuring black female characters to libraries, schools, and community organizations throughout the world.

Reducing Plastic Pollution

Like many other young activists, Dias was amazed by how quickly her dream became reality. High school student Jackson Hinkle had a similar experience at San Clemente High School in San Clemente, California. In 2016 Hinkle, an avid outdoor enthusiast, used Instagram to invite his classmates to join an adventure club that would host hikes, bike rides, and other activities. Hinkle expected around thirty people to respond, but nearly three hundred students showed up for the first meeting. Hinkle says, "At that moment I knew something big could come of it and I didn't want to waste that energy."[10]

The previous year Hinkle had taken part in a volunteer beach cleanup effort and had seen firsthand the mounds of plastic trash

High school–age volunteers take part in a trash cleanup project. After participating in a similar project at a nearby beach, a California high school student organized a group whose focus was to reduce plastic pollution.

collected. He decided to harness the energy of all of those students who had expressed interest in his club by forming the Team Zissou Environmental Organization. The group would focus on reducing plastic pollution. But Hinkle realized he was inexperienced when it came to managing a large group, so he volunteered at a local community service organization in hopes of learning organizational skills. Through his volunteer work for the Ecology Center (an organization that promotes social, agricultural, and environmental change through its focus on community gardening, sensible use of water resources, and healthy eating), Hinkle learned how non-profit organizations work. Most importantly, he gained extensive hands-on knowledge about managing environmental campaigns.

In 2017 Hinkle used his newly acquired skills to launch the Plastic Free initiative at his high school. The project promotes reusable water bottles, which Team Zissou sells on campus. Team Zissou also worked with local delis and other food establishments to encourage them to stop selling water in plastic bottles.

Hinkle did not limit his promotional efforts to social media. In 2018 he wrote an article for the San Clemente High School newspaper. The article explains the importance of the Plastic Free initiative while referencing Hinkle's experience as a volunteer who had helped clean up litter from local beaches:

On Coastal Cleanup Day . . . plastic bottles were the second most found pollutant on our beaches, and plastic bottle caps were the third. In the United States alone, it takes fifteen to seventeen million barrels of oil to manufacture, transport, and dispose of plastic water bottles annually—that's enough to fuel more than 1,000,000 cars for an entire year! Worst of all, scientists estimate that by the year 2050, there will be more plastic in our oceans than fish.[11]

The article announced a Team Zissou student-led campaign, #PlasticFreeCUSD. The project was created in partnership with the Capistrano Unified School District and a company called Just Water, which sells spring water in paper-based cartons with caps made from plant-based materials. The school district launched a pilot program to replace plastic water bottles with Just Water in four schools. Students were so supportive of the measure that the school district eliminated plastic bottles at all of its sixty-four school cafeterias.

While Hinkle was focused on local environmental issues, he also planned to make Plastic Free a global movement. By 2018 Team Zissou had eight high school chapters in California, Hawaii, Washington, and Canada. Hinkle was chosen to be a youth delegate at the Washington Youth Summit on the Environment in Washington, DC. When asked about his future plans, Hinkle has a ready answer: "I want to be President. . . . I want to be someone who makes a lot of positive change in the world. That's just the most powerful way to do it."[12]

While some might scoff at Hinkle's dream, at least one US president began his career as a community activist when he was in his early twenties. Barack Obama worked as a community organizer in Chicago in 1983. As a worker for the Developing Communities Project, Obama helped residents in some of Chicago's poorest neighborhoods fight for better housing and a cleaner environment. In 2007 Obama recalled the experience at a Chicago rally: "It's as a consequence of working with [the project] and this community that I found my calling. There was something more than making money and getting a fancy degree. The measure of my life would be public service."[13]

Eliminating Pesticide Spraying in Parks

When Obama was running for president in 2008, his words and deeds inspired countless others, including Xiuhtezcatl (pronounced shoe-TEZ-caht) Martinez. Although Martinez was only six years old at the time, he used his computer to piece together a video to convince people to vote for Obama. At this time Martinez was already a member of the youth-based conservation organization Earth Guardians. The group was founded by his mother, Tamara Rose, in Boulder, Colorado, in 1992.

Martinez supported Obama because he believed the candidate, if elected, would take steps to slow climate change. He also thought that Obama would inspire young people to get off their couches and work to save the environment. Martinez began giving speeches at Boulder environmental rallies when he was still in first grade. As Martinez recalls in his 2017 memoir, *We Rise*:

When people saw me speak as a little kid, I came across as fiery and determined. I was exposed to such big issues at a young age, and it was a lot for a 6-year-old to come to terms with. . . . [But] during those early days in Boulder, I found one of the most important things a human being can find—my voice. Giving those early speeches motivated me to learn more, because I realized that people would listen and feel inspired when I spoke.[14]

Martinez continued to use his voice to inspire and motivate. At age nine he worked with the Earth Guardians on a project aimed at preventing Boulder officials from spraying pesticides in city parks. Pesticides are used to kill insects that damage plants. Martinez and the others in his group were concerned that these pesticides were poisoning the environment and could even possibly harm kids who play in the park. While other local environmental groups were part of the fight, Martinez helped increase public awareness about the issue by arranging a youth press conference.

To organize the press conference, Martinez visited the websites of local media outlets. He conducted research do discover which newspaper, radio, and TV reporters were interested in environmental issues. He e-mailed the reporters and informed them that the youth press conference would feature fifteen speakers, all of them under age thirteen. The reporters recognized a good story

Teens in the Lead on Climate Change

"We are the ones we've been waiting for." This is the quote that greets visitors to the website of Zero Hour, a youth-led movement for climate and environmental justice. On July 21, 2018, the group marched in Washington DC and other cities. Their goal: To persuade lawmakers to "meaningfully address the climate crisis and protect the future of the youth" and urge other young people to step up and join their cause.

The teen organizers of the group come from different parts of the country. Their planning sessions have taken place mostly through social media. The distances have not deterred them. Besides organizing that first march, they developed a platform and guiding principles. They have met with close to forty lawmakers. This is just the start. "The march is a launch. It isn't, 'That's it, we're done,'" says Zero Hour's founder Jamie Margolin of Seattle, Washington.

Getting started was not easy, but Margolin found inspiration in other recent movements, among them the Women's March and the youth-led March For Our Lives. "No one gives you an organizing guide of how to raise thousands of dollars, how to get people on board, how to mobilize," Margolin says. They are learning as they go, and they are determined to bring about change. Says Margolin, "We are on the verge of something amazing. We're going to change history."

Zero Hour. http://thisiszerohour.org.

Quoted in Alexandra Yoon-Hendricks, "Meet the Teenagers Leading a Climate Change Movement," *New York Times*, July 21, 2018. www.nytimes.com.

in the making—when young people are involved in a community issue, reporters are usually eager to provide coverage. The young activists who held the press conference were well prepared. They had studied research on the danger of the chemicals being used and had learned about safer alternatives.

After successfully fielding questions from the press, Martinez and the Earth Guardians attended a city council meeting, where they planned to tell the mayor and council members about their concerns. Martinez recruited his six-year-old brother, Itzcuauhtli (pronounced eat-SQUAT-lee), to address the city council. The boy had to stand on a box to reach the microphone. He said, "I shouldn't be here right now speaking to you. I should be outside playing in the park. But, because you guys aren't doing your job well, I have to come and tell you how to do it."[15]

The words of this very young activist shocked the elected officials in the room. The Boulder City Council voted to create an Integrated Pest Management plan, which uses nontoxic techniques to reduce the number of pests found in parks. Martinez explains his group's success: "The emotion and the passion we, as kids, brought played a role in getting them to take action. We realized that our size had nothing to do with our ability to effect change."[16]

Holding a Mock Funeral

After their success in Boulder, the young activists continued to meet, raise money, and take action on other environmental issues. In 2013 the group worked locally to address global climate change by rallying to shut down a local coal-fired power plant. At one of their events, the Earth Guardians planted sunflowers at the power plant to symbolize the energy coming from the sun. Power plant employees later killed the sprouting sunflowers by spraying them with herbicides (which are chemicals normally used to kill weeds).

Martinez responded by organizing a mock funeral for the sunflowers. Activists often hold mock funerals as a way to shock the public and attract media attention. Members of the Earth Guardians made large cardboard coffins and painted them black.

Dressed in black, they returned to the power plant, gathered the dying sunflowers, and placed them in the coffins. The activists gathered around the coffins, said prayers for the future, and sang songs. As expected, the event was covered by the local media, which spread word of the protest to the general public. The action, which only required a few buckets of black paint and some recycled cardboard, helped the young activists gather signatures for a petition to shut down the power plant. Several months later, city officials decided to convert the plant from coal to natural gas.

Today, Earth Guardians is one of the largest youth-based environmental organizations in the world, and its leader has never stopped agitating for change. In 2015 Martinez addressed the United Nations General Assembly on climate change, the youngest person to do so. In 2016 he appeared on numerous television shows, including *The Daily Show* and *Real Time with Bill Maher*, to discuss how climate change is affecting his generation and indigenous peoples.

> "I encourage you to be brave about taking your first steps in using your voice for good. . . . The voice of young people is going to be crucial in combating the challenges we face."[17]
>
> —Xiuhtezcatl Martinez, youth director of Earth Guardians

Go Beyond Your Comfort Zone

Dias, Hinkle, and Martinez have found success using some new and some time-honored activist tactics. They utilized the power of social media, convinced friends to join their cause, learned from experienced activists, employed writing skills, contacted reporters, held press conferences, spoke to politicians, and organized public events. All of these activists also recognized that being young can be an advantage. As Martinez advises, "I encourage you to be brave about taking your first steps in using your voice for good. I often see that when we go beyond our comfort zones, the world meets us halfway. The voice of young people is going to be crucial in combating the challenges we face."[17]

CHAPTER 2

Turning Tragedy into Action

> "Be a nuisance where it counts. Do your part to inform and stimulate the public to join your action. Be depressed, discouraged, and disappointed at failure and the disheartening effects of ignorance, greed, corruption and bad politics—but never give up."
>
> —Marjory Stoneman Douglas, writer and conservationist
>
> Quoted in AJ Willingham, "In the Wave of Walkouts, a Quote from Marjory Stoneman Douglas Becomes a Rallying Cry," CNN, March 14, 2018. www.cnn.com.

School shootings have become a sad fact of life in the United States. According to a study by the nonpartisan research group Gun Violence Archive, there were 239 shootings at schools in the United States between the start of 2013 and February 2018. In connection with those shootings, 138 people were killed and about 400 wounded at US elementary schools, middle schools, high schools, colleges, and universities.

The motives of school shooters are often unfathomable. With few answers as to why these senseless killings take place, the public reacts in what journalist Garance Franke-Ruta labels a "template of grief." Calls go out for stronger gun control laws on the one hand and the arming of teachers on the other. The motives of the shooter are analyzed. Some blame mental illness or violent video games and movies. Franke-Ruta fleshes out the template of grief idea: "Survivors speak. . . . People leave piles of flowers and teddy bears at the shooting site. There are candlelight vigils, and teary memorials. Everyone calls for national unity and a moment of togetherness."[18]

Media coverage of a mass shooting usually tapers off after about five days, and the public tends to lose interest. As mass shootings become more frequent, people become desensitized. They experience disaster fatigue: Anger fades into helplessness, people assume nothing will change, and many try to tune out the bad news. Psychologist Michael Unger explains disaster fatigue by saying that when another "tragedy strikes (it is only a matter of time before the next mass shooting occurs), more anger erupts, more helplessness follows. . . . The desire to advocate for change fades and is replaced by two emotions. First, resignation, or emotional withdrawal. Second, bitterness."[19]

Planning a Campaign

There was little reason to think that the public response would be much different after fourteen students and three staff members were killed at Marjory Stoneman Douglas (MSD) High School in Parkland, Florida, on February 14, 2018. But student activists at the school were determined to shatter the template of grief and shake people out of their disaster fatigue. Choking back tears, MSD high school senior Emma González spoke at a Tallahassee, Florida, gun control rally three days after the shooting. González made it clear that the student-led movement was not going to fade away:

> "If you actively do nothing, people will continually end up dead so it's time to start doing something. . . . We are going to be the last mass shooting."[20]
>
> —Emma González, joint founder of the Never Again movement

Maybe the adults have gotten used to saying, "It is what it is." But if us students have learned anything, it's that if you do not study, you will fail. And this case, if you actively do nothing, people will continually end up dead so it's time to start doing something. We are going to be the kids you read about in textbooks. Not because we're going to be another statistic about mass shooting in America, but because . . . we are going to be the last mass shooting.[20]

González's eloquent speech went viral and helped put a face to the student gun control movement that was rapidly expanding in Parkland. As often happens with social movements that spread via social media, a dizzying number of events occurred almost simultaneously. González had already joined a small group of MSD students that had come together the previous day to organize a social movement. The group was making plans to hold large demonstrations to pressure politicians to support gun control measures. The group, described by journalist Lisa Miller as "theater geeks and drama nerds and journalism fanatics,"[21] also included Sarah Chadwick, Jaclyn Corin, Alex Wind, and David Hogg. Group member Cameron Kasky came up with the hashtag #NeverAgain, which gave a name to the movement.

Using Everyone's Special Skills

Each member of the Never Again movement brought special skills to group. González, who identifies as bisexual, had been the president of the high school's Gay-Straight Alliance (GSA) for three years. The GSA is a community-based organization active in hundreds of middle schools, high schools, colleges, and universities. González says being her school's GSA president helped her sharpen her activist skills: "It's really helped me get used to shifting plans very quickly, planning in advance, and also being flexible."[22]

As junior-class president, Corin was familiar with the dynamics of running a small-scale political campaign. Her leadership skills came into play when she organized the bus trip that took González and another one hundred MSD students to the February 17 Tallahassee rally.

Hogg honed his media talents as a junior reporter for the *Sun Sentinel*, a local newspaper. After the shooting he put his journalistic skills to work by interviewing student survivors and relating their stories to journalists and talk show hosts. Kasky, a member of the high school drama club, created some memorable drama when he took on Florida senator Marco Rubio during a February 22 "Stand Up" town hall sponsored by CNN. Rubio had taken more than $3.3

million from the National Rifle Association (NRA) during his career, and Kasky repeatedly implored the senator to stop taking donations from the pro-gun group. When Rubio refused to do so, Kasky received thunderous applause when he compared the senator to the type of gun used in the MSD shooting: "Senator Rubio, it's hard to look at you and not look down a barrel of an AR-15."[23] Rubio did not respond directly to Kasky's comment. Instead, he encouraged the young activist to continue to work toward change.

Dunking, Burning, and Owning on Twitter

Kasky and others were criticized by some for being too abrasive and confrontational. But they were speaking in the language of a generation raised on social media, where terms like *dunk*, *burn*, and *own* are commonly used to describe winning an argument.

The Words That Caught the World's Attention

On February 17, 2018, MSD senior Emma González gave a speech at a Ft. Myers, Florida, gun control rally. During the emotional twelve-minute speech, González called out elected officials who take money from the NRA. Her goal was to shame those officials into rejecting the NRA money or persuade voters to vote them out of office. To make sure that her message resonated long after the speech had ended, González decided to repeat three simple words throughout her speech: "We call BS." (She said later that she did not want to use the actual word because she knew children would be listening.) The crowd responded by shouting those words back at her each time she said them. Below is an excerpt of her speech.

> Politicians who sit in their gilded House and Senate seats funded by the NRA telling us nothing could have been done to prevent this. We call BS. They say tougher guns laws do not decrease gun violence. We call BS. They say a good guy with a gun stops a bad guy with a gun. We call BS. They say guns are just tools like knives and are as dangerous as cars. We call BS. They say no laws could have prevented the hundreds of senseless tragedies that have occurred. We call BS. That us kids don't know what we're talking about, that we're too young to understand how the government works. We call BS.

Quoted in CNN, "Florida Student Emma Gonzalez to Lawmakers and Gun Advocates: 'We Call BS,'" February 17, 2018. www.cnn.com.

Chadwick was particularly skilled at using sarcasm and satire to dunk, burn, and own. As she tweeted after the February 22 "Stand Up": "We should change the names of AR-15s to 'Marco Rubios' because they are so easy to buy."[24] The comment was quickly retweeted 73,000 times and liked by 293,000 people. Chadwick soon had over 150,000 Twitter followers. Her comment was also mentioned by late-night talk show host Seth Meyers, who called the tweet a "white-hot burn."[25]

As their cause attracted greater attention, the MSD activists continued to prove their mastery of Twitter by racking up followers. Two weeks after the shooting, Chadwick and Hogg had each amassed more than 320,000 followers, and González, with 955,000 followers, had nearly twice as many as the NRA.

Reaching for the Next Level

The MSD students took advantage of their growing presence on social media to recruit like-minded peers. The Never Again campaign grew to about twenty students locally, and the group gathered at Kasky's house to take the movement to the national level. The students decided early on to remain nonpartisan; although 98 percent of NRA political contributions go to Republican politicians, the activists did not want to alienate millions of Republicans who might otherwise be sympathetic to their cause.

They also knew the importance of media exposure. Even before the shooting, most of the students behind the Never Again campaign were avid consumers of news. They watched cable news, listened to public radio, surfed Internet news sites, and were active on social media platforms. They understood that the media would quickly tire of interviewing the same three or four people, so they picked a dozen or so students who would split up media assignments. As Corin explains, "We knew our places. . . . David focuses on the hard facts. Cameron is sarcastic and witty. Emma's strong. I'm more of an organizer. Alex is the emotional remembrance of it all. Alfonso Calderon does all the Spanish interviews."[26]

> "David focuses on the hard facts. Cameron is sarcastic and witty. Emma's strong. I'm more of an organizer. . . . Alfonso Calderon does all the Spanish interviews."[26]
>
> —Jaclyn Corin, joint founder of the Never Again movement

United Around a Message

The students also understood that if they were to launch a successful campaign, they would need to unite around a strong message. This would prevent them from possibly saying the wrong thing or contradicting one another when interviewed. They created a focused five-step agenda that could be endorsed by politicians and supported by the public. The agenda was based on exacting research conducted by Never Again members. For example, they knew that Congress passed an NRA-backed amendment in 1996 to prevent the Centers for Disease Control and Prevention from conducting research into gun violence. The Never Again group wanted this amendment repealed. The group's agenda also called for all records of gun sales to be digitized; as it stands now, gun sales are recorded on paper forms, which are extremely hard to search when authorities want to track weapons used in crimes. The students called for universal background checks on gun buyers and limits on high-capacity magazines, which allow a single shooter to fire up to thirty bullets before reloading. The ultimate demand, a ban on all assault weapons, was also included in the group's agenda.

Although these five points helped the student activists stay focused, these proposed measures were by no means new. Gun control supporters had been advocating similar actions for years; gun control opponents had honed their arguments against these actions during that same time period. This made some of the points politically toxic. To counter this phenomenon, the Never Again activists carefully refined their message by choosing words that would have the most impact in the media. They sat together in a circle and wrote popular words—called buzzwords—that would be particularly effective. The list of buzzwords included *reform*, *change*, *safety*, *children*, and *innocents*. With buzzwords in hand, the group members rehearsed responses they would give to those who disagreed with them.

A Mission Statement and a March

Having completed the work to present a unified front to the media, the Never Again activists announced their plans for a wave of national demonstrations. The March For Our Lives rally was planned for March 24 in Washington, DC, and in hundreds of other cities around the world. Additionally, the activists called for the Enough! National School Walkout to be held on two dates. The March 14 walkout was on the one-month anniversary of the Parkland shooting, while the April 20 walkout commemorated the 1999 Columbine High School massacre in Colorado.

During a 2018 rally in Ft. Lauderdale, Florida, MSD high school senior, David Hogg, urges lawmakers to pass gun control measures. Hogg was one of the student organizers of the #NeverAgain movement.

The group promoted the March For Our Lives event with a sophisticated social media campaign. Group members created a website and opened accounts for the march on Facebook, Twitter, Instagram, and other sites. Tumblr was particularly important to the activists. They used the site to create a "protest art pack" that included stickers, GIFs, and illustrations for others to use to decorate their blogs and social media pages. The group's Tumblr Action page featured information on how to create and sign petitions calling for gun safety, as well as voter registration forms for those who would turn eighteen before the next election.

In order to encourage companion rallies on March 24, the activists created an eighteen-page tool kit and made it available online. The tool kit highlights a three-step process others could follow:

STEP 1: Planning a March in Your Community
STEP 2: Publicize Your March: Build Awareness and Recruit!
STEP 3: The Day of the March: How to Have a Powerful Event.[27]

Creating a Bold Mission Statement

Activist groups have long used mission statements to articulate their goals. In February 2018, when the Parkland activists announced the March 24 March For Our Lives rally, they issued a bold mission statement. The statement, excerpted below, clearly and concisely describes their goals.

Not one more. We cannot allow one more child to be shot at school. We cannot allow one more teacher to make a choice to jump in front of an assault rifle to save the lives of students. We cannot allow one more family to wait for a call or text that never comes. Our children and teachers are dying. We must make it our top priority to save these lives. . . .

The mission and focus of March For Our Lives is to assure that no special interest group or political agenda is more critical than timely passage of legislation to effectively address the gun violence issues that are rampant in our country. We demand morally-just leaders to rise up from both parties in order to ensure public safety.

Specifically, we are working towards . . .

Universal, comprehensive background checks

Bringing the ATF into the 21st century with a digitized, searchable database

Funds for the Center[s] for Disease Control to research the gun violence epidemic in America

High-capacity magazine ban

Assault weapons ban. . . .

We will not stop our advocacy until we see the change we demand—a change that is necessary in order to save innocent lives across our nation.

March For Our Lives, "Mission Statement," 2018. https://marchforourlives.com.

The tool kit provides extensive information that students can use to promote any cause. It features sample tweets and Facebook posts, graphics, and templates for letters designed to inform local media outlets about the march.

The Never Again activists also turned to crowdsourcing for help. They raised money through a GoFundMe campaign, and the response was overwhelming. Within three days the group brought in $1.7 million in small donations. By mid-March that number had more than doubled to $3.5 million. The group brought in another $2 million from high-profile celebrities, including Oprah Winfrey, George Clooney, and Steven Spielberg. The funds were used to pay for supplies and equipment and to coordinate the Washington, DC, demonstration. The group's profile was further raised when its efforts were recognized by Barack Obama, who tweeted: "Young people have helped lead all our great movements. How inspiring to see it again in so many smart, fearless students standing up for their right to be safe; marching and organizing to remake the world as it should be. We've been waiting for you. And we've got your backs."[28]

Lobbying Politicians

As momentum built for the national march, the students continued to pressure their home state politicians. Some visited legislators in the Florida state capital of Tallahassee and lobbied them to pass gun control measures. At first this seemed like an impossible task. Between 2010 and 2018, the NRA spent more than $8 million lobbying Florida politicians to loosen gun laws. During that time, lawmakers passed some of the most relaxed gun regulations in the country. Pro–gun rights Florida legislators were proud of their work. They often highlighted their A+ rating from the NRA in speeches and campaign commercials. But as the 2018 election approached, that NRA rating lost a little bit of its luster. As González stated, "We keep telling [the politicians] that if they accept this [NRA] blood money, they are against the children, they are against the people who are dying. We are not forgetting this come [the 2018] midterm elections."[29]

Pressure by González and others in the Never Again movement helped convince some of the politicians to back modest gun control measures. On March 7, 2018, the Republican majority in the Florida House of Representatives passed legislation to raise the age to purchase firearms from eighteen to twenty-one. The law imposed a three-day waiting period on some firearms purchases and gave law enforcement more authority to seize weapons from those deemed mentally unfit. The activists wanted a ban on assault weapons, which they did not get, but many were pleased by the passage of the gun control measures.

Joining with Others

The victory in the legislature helped fuel excitement for the March For Our Lives rally. But the students knew that if the march was to be successful, they would need help from partner organizations. The activists joined forces with the gun control group Giffords, associated with former Arizona representative Gabrielle Giffords, who survived a Tucson shooting in 2011. Never Again also partnered with Everytown for Gun Safety, which organized the March 24 rallies in Atlanta, Chicago, Las Vegas, and elsewhere. Everytown handed out $5,000 grants to over two hundred community organizations throughout the country so they could join in the March For Our Lives event. Entertainers were eager to volunteer, and performers such as Miley Cyrus, Common, Demi Lovato, and Ariana Grande stepped forward to entertain the crowd in Washington, DC.

The March For Our Lives rally was an overwhelming success. Over half a million people attended the main event in Washington, DC. Thousands more took part in similar rallies around the United States and in cities worldwide, including Tokyo, Rome, and London. But even after the rallies focused international attention on gun control, the students behind #NeverAgain made it clear that their goal was not a single successful march. The activists want lawmakers across the nation to enact gun laws, and most were committed to putting in whatever time and effort was necessary to achieve that goal.

Toward this end, the activists set up a media lab in a nondescript Parkland strip mall after the march. The lab became a hive of activity as students worked to produce memes and video content meant to keep the gun control issue in the public eye. As MSD alumnus Leslie Chiu put it: "This is not a moment. This is a movement."[30] The movement was kept alive by media lab videos created to explain the politics of gun control, the history of gun violence, and the importance of voting.

While the #NeverAgain activists were motivated by a tragedy, they reacted with tools available to all students—and to all Americans. They lobbied politicians, spoke to reporters, gave speeches, and used the Internet to build support for their cause. Students who feel strongly about an issue in their schools, their communities, their states, the nation, or the world can also bring about change. They do not have to experience a terrible event to act. That is one of the benefits of living in a democracy: Student activists who want to bring about change can have a lasting impact.

> "This is not a moment. This is a movement."[30]
> —Leslie Chiu, MSD alumnus

CHAPTER 3

Taking Action

> "I believe that my generation has the power to change the world more than any group before us. Unlike the generations in decades past, we have more information available to us than ever before. . . . With the click of a button, our words can be shared with millions."
>
> —Jordyn I., New Jersey high school student
>
> Quoted in Katherine Schulten, "The Power to Change the World: A Teaching Unit on Student Activism in History and Today," *New York Times*, March 15, 2018. www.nytimes.com.

Every day, student activists take on problems at all levels of society. They start individual programs or work through their local scout troop or religious institution. Some sign up to work with national organizations. Whatever the course of action, the activists are motivated to take on matters they feel are being ignored. Instead of waiting for someone else to fix a problem, the activists follow the advice of Marley Dias: "Identify the issues in your community you think are unfair, then take action to change them."[31]

That is good advice, but creating change is not always easy. Commitment to a cause involves hard work, patience, and passion. Some causes are controversial and require student activists to face off against a strong, well-organized opposition. And success is never guaranteed. But even if you find yourself taking one step backward for every two steps forward, you can overcome many obstacles if you apply the tactics developed over the years by those who have succeeded.

Know Your Issue

Many student-led campaigns begin when one person sees an injustice or a need at school or in the community. The student might not know exactly how to change the situation; he or she just knows that *something* needs to be done. As self-help author Stephen R. Covey writes, most people have a deep-rooted desire to help: "Our basic nature is to act, and not be acted upon. . . . Taking initiative does not mean being pushy, obnoxious, or aggressive. It does mean recognizing our responsibility to make things happen."[32]

When activists want to make things happen, the first step is learning everything there is to know about the issue. The youth activism manual published by the Tennessee chapter of the American Civil Liberties Union (ACLU) explains why research is important, even if it seems like an extra homework assignment: "The value of information cannot be overstated. Research is vital not only for figuring out good solutions, but also for establishing support for your cause. Knowing your issue inside and out and backing up your arguments will help people understand why this issue merits action."[33] The ACLU is a nationwide organization whose focus is the defense and preservation of individual rights and liberties guaranteed by the Constitution and other laws.

> "Our basic nature is to act, and not be acted upon. . . . Taking initiative . . . [means] recognizing our responsibility to make things happen."[32]
>
> —Stephen R. Covey, self-help author

An efficient way to conduct research is to find answers to questions reporters refer to as the "five Ws": who, what, why, where, and when. This is what one group of students did when they learned about budget cuts at their school. In 2016 a small group of high school students at Snowden International School in Boston decided to learn more about plans to cut foreign language classes throughout the school district due to a budget shortfall.

Through their research, the Snowden students learned that the decision was made by Boston Public Schools officials. The students also learned that in addition to foreign language programs being dropped as a result of the budget cuts, several popular teachers would lose their jobs. As students struggled to understand the cuts, they learned that the district was facing an

$18 million shortfall. The money was being used to fund charter schools, private institutions that receive government funding but operate independently. The students found where they could voice their concerns; a state house hearing on school budget issues was being held in the coming days. So student activists made plans to testify about how the budget cuts would affect their education. They found out when to be there. They also organized a school walkout shortly before politicians voted on the cuts.

In March 2016 over thirty-five hundred Boston students left their classrooms and marched through the streets to protest the school budget cuts. Senior Jahi Spaloss explained what drove her to participate in the walkout: "There's this stereotype that young kids don't know what we're doing and should let adults handle things because it's their fight more than ours. But we're the ones in school. This fight is ours."[34] The fight continued into 2017, when Boston mayor Marty Walsh, who was running for reelection, agreed to increase funding for city schools by $29 million.

The Boston students, like many activists, began their research on the Internet—they just started googling. For just about any issue that concerns you, you are likely to find information on hundreds (or even thousands) of websites. But searching all of those sites is a waste of time. The Internet is teeming with rumors, gossip, and outright lies meant to sway public opinion. The key to a fruitful search is to start by looking at the source of the information. Interested organizations, news media, nonpartisan research groups, and government agencies often provide reliable information. But even then, it is advisable to double-check your facts. See if you can find the same information on more than one website. Activists should avoid citing memes, conspiracy websites, biased blogs, and other questionable sources. In this era of intense political division, it is helpful to find neutral sources. For example, a government study on the effects of air pollution on childhood asthma might have more credibility among the general public than a study funded by a large environmental organiza-

A Google search is a good place to begin when researching an issue, but student activists should always double check their facts before speaking out. It is also important to consider the sources of the information and how credible they are.

tion with a political agenda. As the ACLU explains, "Be aware that different segments of the public may perceive some media sources or interest-driven organizations as more or less credible than others. Your source of information can make or break whether someone sees your argument as legitimate."[35]

Build a Team

After completing your research you should decide whether you want to address an issue by yourself or build a team to tackle the problem. While working alone can be efficient, there is power in numbers.

"Social activism is supposed to be just that: social! . . . Surround yourself with as many cheerleaders as you can get because keeping your confidence up is half the battle."[36]

—Marley Dias, founder of the #1000BlackGirlBooks campaign

As Dias writes, "Social activism is supposed to be just that: social! . . . Surround yourself with as many cheerleaders as you can get because keeping your confidence up is half the battle."[36]

The first team-building step is to recruit a core group of people with similar beliefs. Ideally, this inner circle will include three

Branding a Campaign

Student activists who want their events to resonate with the public need to create a brand for their campaign. This involves producing symbols, catchphrases, and logos. All are meant to work together to create a memorable public image for the group. There is even an app for that: WalkWoke was launched in 2018 by Tangelo, an innovation design lab founded by immigrant women. The WalkWoke app lets users create posters that can be used as digital artwork on social media sites. The posters can also be printed out as flyers or full-size for use at marches. The templates, created by professional artists, cover several dozen causes, including climate change, freedom of speech, immigrants' rights, and environmental justice. Users can customize their posters by choosing artistic backgrounds, fonts, type sizes, and colors. As a user named Tara C. noted, "WalkWoke has made it so easy for me to create posters [even without having an] artistic background! They have an awesome number of templates you can choose from."

Quoted in WalkWoke, "Stand Up for Equality and Justice for All," 2018. www.walkwoke.com.

to seven students who have a variety of talents. Activist groups need good speakers and people with writing skills and leadership abilities. Those with strong community connections help group members find a shared sense of purpose. Activists need passion for the cause and patience and determination to persist against opponents and obstruction (if either of these arise). Students also need to commit their time; activist groups often meet at night and on weekends when others are playing video games, eating, and sleeping. #NeverAgain member Delaney Tarr tweeted about the hardships of life as a dedicated activist. She often eats crackers for dinner and stays up late into the night as she works for the gun control cause. As Tarr acknowledges, "This is not a sprint. This is a marathon. This is something we have to keep working on for months, for years even."[37]

Crackers for dinner and little sleep should not be the norm. To work on projects for any length of time, activists

> "This is not a sprint. This is a marathon. This is something we have to keep working on for months, for years even."[37]
>
> —Delaney Tarr, Never Again activist

have to take care of their health by eating properly and sleeping enough. And time can be better managed if a group delegates tasks and assigns leaders for specific roles. For example, one person should be assigned to work as a media coordinator to interact with reporters and the public. The job requires someone who can shape a group's message into a set of consistent talking points. Media coordinators are also in charge of the very important task of managing social media, which can help launch a campaign when done properly—or kill one when mismanaged.

Most activist projects need a recruitment coordinator to attract supporters to the campaign. Recruitment coordinators put up flyers, speak to community groups, and search for like-minded activists on social media. Recruitment coordinators also manage inexperienced volunteers, who perform tasks such as making phone calls, creating signs, and maintaining websites.

Team building is an important step in organizing for a cause. During the school year, most of this activity takes place on nights and weekends.

The secretary-treasurer of a group plays another important role. This job involves taking minutes at meetings, answering mail and e-mails, and managing whatever funds are raised by a group. The secretary-treasurer works closely with the project's chair, who provides leadership for the group. As the campaign's "chief executive officer," the chair makes sure meetings are orderly and conducted efficiently and that everyone's voice is heard. The chair works as a strategist to plan long-term goals for the project and ensures that the goals set by the group are carried out. The chair supervises other senior members of the team and often represents the group at functions and media events.

Fund-raising events and public demonstrations need additional planners. An event producer ensures that a stage, podium, and sound system are available and, if needed, hires a local ven-

Getting the Most Out of Social Media

Social media sites such as Facebook, Instagram, Twitter, and Tumblr are extremely valuable activist tools. The sites allow groups to recruit new members, keep current members informed, and publicize direct action events. Activists who wish to reach as many people as possible can do several things to increase their success on social media.

When inviting people to an event, provide a way for them to RSVP, or respond to the invitation. This confirms that they will be attending. The RSVP can include a link to your group's website or Facebook page. Once people respond, you can send them e-mails to remind them of an action and request their attendance at other events. A group can also set up a number for text messaging using a unique code that reflects its activist message. Those who respond can receive information about local rallies.

Social media postings should also encourage supporters to use the group's hashtag as often as possible. This helps organizers search for content related to their activities. Hashtags also help promote an activist project to a national audience while effectively showing how much public support is behind the cause.

While social media has revolutionized activism, there is also a downside. People can spread misinformation about a cause or start online feuds that distract from the message. Therefore, it is important for a media coordinator to keep a watchful eye on a group's postings and take antihacking measures when necessary.

dor to provide a public address system and other equipment. An event coordinator checks with police or city officials to find out whether permits are needed or seeks permission from school officials for events to be held on campus. Large events might require some form of security; a security coordinator checks on this before the event. For a rally, a program coordinator contacts speakers, takes care of travel arrangements, acts as an emcee, and organizes entertainment.

Many student activists have benefited from getting help from adults when planning an event. Those who planned the Boston high school walkout worked with adult allies, who created an online petition to gather support for the demonstration. The students also worked with the advocacy group Boston Education Justice Alliance, which provided poster boards and markers to make signs. The alliance also provided snacks and drinks to students who worked long hours to plan the event. Dias explains the importance of working with grown-ups: "I've relied a lot on adults for guidance and have let them show me the best ways to be an activist, and stay safe while doing it. A word of advice: If you're a kid like me, I recommend doing the same thing. Get adults to help you. After all, they're bigger, louder, and can get other adults to be on your team."[38]

Direct Action

After research and team building are done, it is time to take the campaign public with direct action. The type of action a group takes will depend on the cause. If students are trying to change a school policy, they should plan to first take their case to school administrators. Depending on the outcome, the next step might be to attend a school board meeting. (People who wish to speak at public meetings often need to sign up ahead of time. And speakers often have time limits for their comments. These are details worth checking on.) The spokesperson must be prepared to express the group's concerns clearly and succinctly.

In 2018 a small group of students in Memphis, Tennessee, organized to urge the local school board to not arm teachers. The school board was considering a plan to allow some teachers to keep guns in classrooms to ward off a possible mass shooting. Student organizers met the weekend before the school board meeting to make a list of alternatives. The suggestions included adding mental health and conflict-resolution classes and making more time for teachers to have one-on-one sessions with troubled students. After meeting with the students, school superintendent Dorsey Hopson said he was very impressed with their efforts. The school district took the students' suggestions into account, along with other concerns, when it decided to hire more school resource officers rather than arm teachers.

Did the Action Work?

When the student activists in Memphis met after their action, they evaluated their efforts and celebrated their success. Evaluating the effectiveness of the campaign is always a good idea. Did the activity raise awareness or cause a policy to be changed? Did the group attract followers on social media sites, or was it largely ignored? In what ways could the activist project be fine-tuned to attract more attention?

A campaign might achieve minor changes or become a huge success with supporters that continue to work on the cause for months or even years. Whatever happens, activism can be fun and exciting. It is a great learning experience and a way to develop lifelong friendships. Changing people's behavior is not easy, and there are many obstacles to moving the world in a positive direction. But everyone has a right to have his or her voice heard, and activists have achieved success with ten people as well as ten thousand. If students see a problem, there is no need to wait for others to take action. As Dias says, "Be the change you want to see in the world."[39]

CHAPTER 4

Know Your Rights

"In our system . . . school officials do not possess absolute authority over their students. Students in school, as well as out of school, are 'persons' under our Constitution. . . . Students are entitled to freedom of expression of their views."

—Abe Fortas, Supreme Court justice (1965–1969)

Abe Fortas, *Tinker v. Des Moines Independent Community School Dist.*, 393 U.S. 503 (1969).

In 1965 there was a growing student protest movement in the United States calling for an end to the Vietnam War. Student protesters sometimes wore black armbands to school to show their opposition to the war. In Des Moines, Iowa, thirteen-year-old Mary Beth Tinker joined a small group of middle school students who planned to do just that. But the Des Moines school board heard about their plans and passed a preemptive ban on black armbands.

Tinker, her brother John, and several other students defied the ban and were suspended when they refused to remove their armbands. On their behalf, the ACLU filed a complaint in US District Court. The ACLU argued that the school district infringed on the students' First Amendment right to free speech. The case *Tinker v. Des Moines Independent Community School District* wound its way through the court system for several years. When *Tinker* was finally heard by the US Supreme Court in 1969, the court ruled 7–2 that there was no age limit on the First Amendment guarantee of free speech. The majority opinion, written by Justice Abe Fortas, has been quoted many times since it was written. Part of that opinion states: "It can hardly be argued that . . . [students] shed their constitutional rights to freedom of speech or expression at the schoolhouse gate."[40]

The *Tinker* Test

While the court determined that students in public schools have certain rights, there are limits; speech can be restricted if it is disruptive to normal school activities. The *Tinker* ruling even included a criterion, or standard, to help school officials determine whether an activity is disruptive. Formally known as the substantial disruption test, the criterion is commonly referred to as the *Tinker* test. School officials use the *Tinker* test to answer a question posed by the court: Does the speech or expression of the student "interfere with the . . . appropriate discipline in the operation of the school?"[41] In other words, do the actions of the student hamper the activities of teachers or students or prevent others from learning?

> "It can hardly be argued that . . . [students] shed their constitutional rights to freedom of speech or expression at the school-house gate."[40]
>
> —Abe Fortas, Supreme Court justice from 1965 to 1969

Behaviors that fail the *Tinker* test include handing out protest flyers during class time, standing on a desk and yelling comments about a political issue, or blocking hallways or doorways to protest.

In 2006 the Ninth Circuit Court of Appeals clarified the *Tinker* test by addressing issues that were not considered in the 1960s. Its ruling said that schools can also prohibit student expression if it is considered sexual harassment or hate speech. In the case *Harper v. Poway Unified School District*, the court ruled that school officials could stop a student from wearing a T-shirt that contained biblical verses condemning homosexuality. The student involved believed that he was making a political statement against the expansion of LGBTQ rights. However, a teacher asked the student to remove the shirt, since it was creating a distraction in class and had led to fights in the hallway. The appellate court ruling states, "Speech that attacks high school

If You Are Suspended for Political Activity

Students who participate in school walkouts can be suspended for truancy. All public schools are required by law to provide students with a code of conduct that explains disciplinary procedures and violations that may result in suspension. Carefully reviewing the school's code of conduct before joining a walkout is a good idea.

When students are suspended, the school is required to immediately notify a parent or guardian with a mailed or hand-delivered notice. The notice should contain a detailed description of the violation and an explanation of the student's rights. Students generally have a legal right to challenge what they believe is an unfair suspension. This usually entails a conference with the school principal. Students may bring an attorney or trusted adult to the meeting, and that person may request that the suspension be shortened or canceled. If the conference does not have a satisfactory outcome for the students, they can appeal the disciplinary action before the school board. If the decision goes against the students again, they might be able to appeal to the commissioner of education, a state official who oversees public schools.

students who are members of minority groups that have historically been oppressed, subjected to verbal and physical abuse, and made to feel inferior, serves to injure and intimidate them, as well as to damage their sense of security and interfere with their opportunity to learn."[42]

Courts have clarified the free speech rights of students. But teachers and school officials are sometimes influenced by personal feelings when applying the *Tinker* test to real-world situations. For example, a teacher who agrees with a student protest might view it as protected speech, while a teacher who disagrees with a student's political message might view the protest as disruptive.

There is another limitation concerning student free speech rights. The court rulings only cover public schools, which are government entities. Private schools, which are run by private institutions, do not have the same protections. The First Amendment was created by nation's the founders to limit the power of government. For this reason, the rulings on student free speech rights only apply to public schools.

Student Walkouts

One action that is not protected by the First Amendment, the courts have said, is a student walkout. In a walkout, students stand and leave their classrooms en masse at a given time or signal. This form of protest made headlines in 2018 when the Never Again activists organized the national school walkouts for March 14 and April 20. The events were held to protest the inaction of Congress on the issue of gun violence. Walkout organizers called for students to leave class for seventeen minutes, one minute for each death in the mass shooting at MSD in Parkland, Florida.

Unless there is an emergency, walking out of class in the middle of the school day is considered truancy. Courts have ruled that there is no constitutional right to violate truancy policies. Students can be disciplined for missing class—even if they are protesting issues that are important to them. The punishment for truancy differs by state and even by school district. However, the penalty must adhere to a standard called "content neutral." This

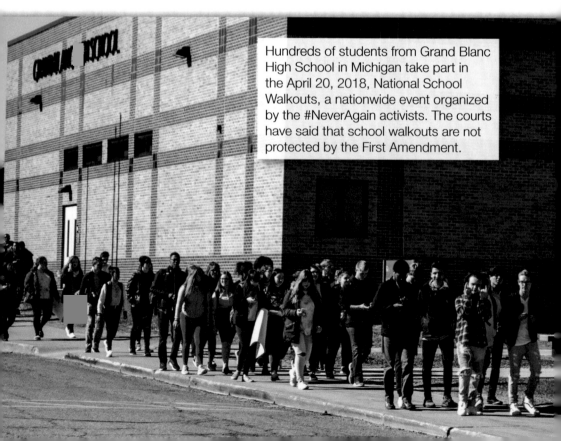

Hundreds of students from Grand Blanc High School in Michigan take part in the April 20, 2018, National School Walkouts, a nationwide event organized by the #NeverAgain activists. The courts have said that school walkouts are not protected by the First Amendment.

means every student who walks out of class receives the same punishment; students cannot receive harsher punishment if they are expressing a political point of view. However, students who have committed previous offenses unrelated to political protest can receive harsher punishment.

Whatever a school's policy, talking ahead of time with school administrators is always advisable. In some cases administrators might be willing to work with students. But that does not always happen.

> "No student will be disciplined because they expressed any particular viewpoint or opinion. . . . [The punishment] will be given for willfully breaking a school rule."[43]
>
> —Jacqueline Rattigan, school superintendent

Tens of thousands of students at an estimated twenty-five hundred US schools took part in the National School Walkouts on March 14. In Park Hill, Kansas, 150 students were ordered to serve detention for their participation in the walkout. At Pennridge High School in East Rock Hill, Pennsylvania, around 225 students who walked out—some accompanied by their parents—were given weekend detention. School superintendent Jacqueline Rattigan explained the policy: "Just to be clear, no student will be disciplined because they expressed any particular viewpoint or opinion. Rather, the disciplinary consequence will be given for willfully breaking a school rule about leaving the building without permission."[43]

The situation was different in New York City, where school officials said walkout participants would be marked absent but not suspended. Around one hundred thousand students who participated in the walkout were joined by New York governor Andrew M. Cuomo and other prominent politicians. In Washington, DC, around three thousand student protesters gathered in front of the White House, where they were joined by politicians who supported their cause. Students who missed class were marked for an unexcused absence or faced lunch detention but received no further penalties. However, those who took part in the walkout were not allowed to make up graded assignments that were given out during class that day.

Rights on Social Media

While officials can regulate student behavior on campus and during the school day, they have no legal right to control student speech outside of school hours. This includes the right to post political views on social media. However, since the early 2010s numerous school districts throughout the country have hired private firms that use advanced software to monitor the posting activities of students. Technology that picks out keywords and phrases has been used to justify punishment of students who engage in online bullying or use abusive language. Supporters of this policy hope that technology can prevent behavior that leads to altercations—or even shootings—at school. However, civil rights and online privacy organizations believe off-campus monitoring infringes on student civil rights. As ACLU attorney Chad Marlow explains, "Schools need to think about, how do we take on these issues in an appropriate way that doesn't have . . . the collateral damage effect of destroying students' privacy and free speech rights? . . . Once you start policing and punishing thoughts, you are into very, very dangerous territory."[44]

> "Once you start policing and punishing thoughts, you are into very, very dangerous territory."[44]
>
> —Chad Marlow, ACLU attorney

It is easy to understand why officials want to keep tabs on social media. According to a 2018 survey by the Pew Research Center, 94 percent of teens say they go online every day, and nearly half are online almost constantly. There is little doubt that Snapchat, Twitter, and other sites have extended the boundaries of the schoolyard. School officials say they are concerned with safety. For this reason, students have been punished for comments made in private online chats that others made public. Some have been reprimanded for forwarding racist posts, even if they were doing so to condemn the words.

While the courts have not ruled on the legality of schools monitoring social media, students should keep the *Harper* case in mind. Schools cannot punish students for political speech, but

Rights When Photographing Police Actions

All Americans have a constitutional right to photograph or videotape the police, government authorities, and anything else that is within public view. This right has taken on great importance in the wake of recent police shootings of young, unarmed black men. There are exceptions to this right. Police can legally order citizens to cease any activity that is interfering with law enforcement operations. Photographers may not place themselves between police and suspects or impede the movements of law officers.

If you are stopped or detained for taking photographs, never resist a police officer physically. Be polite, remain calm, and do not attempt to explain your rights to the police. The ACLU recommends that you ask only one question: "Am I free to go?" Until you ask to leave, your stop is considered voluntary and is legal. If the officer says no, then you are being detained. To detain you, the police must have a reasonable suspicion that you have committed a crime or are about to. Politely ask what crime you are suspected of committing. At this time you can remind the officer that taking photographs is a First Amendment right and does not constitute criminal behavior.

speech with the potential to violate the rights of others is not protected. And anyone who uses social media should assume that their postings are being monitored—and nothing posted online will remain secret forever. But the extent to which school authorities can monitor and punish the online speech of students remains unsettled. This issue will continue to be the focus of court cases in the foreseeable future.

Know Your Rights at a Demonstration

While student rights in the digital world remain in flux, those who gather in public places to peacefully express political viewpoints are guaranteed rights granted to all Americans, regardless of age. However, police sometimes violate these rights through mass arrest, use of force, and attempts to make a protest seem like a criminal act. For this reason it is important for students to know their rights when participating in public demonstrations.

Legal experts say activists of all ages have the right to speak, chant, sing, and march on what are called "public forums." These places include public parks, city streets, and sidewalks. Activists cannot block building entrances or impede or detain pedestrians. However, it is legal to approach pedestrians to offer them a flyer, ask them to sign petitions, or ask for donations for a political cause. In some places a permit is required if activists wish to set up a table for these activities. Protesters cannot march or hand out flyers on private property unless the owner grants permission. Those who attempt to hold a rally on private property, such as an apartment complex or strip mall, can be arrested for trespassing.

Courts have ruled that authorities can restrict the exercise of First Amendment rights according to strict "time, place, and

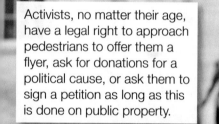

Activists, no matter their age, have a legal right to approach pedestrians to offer them a flyer, ask for donations for a political cause, or ask them to sign a petition as long as this is done on public property.

manner" policies. For example, officials can require protesters to obtain permits for large groups using a public park. They can also place limits on the hours that the protest is allowed to occur and on the volume of public address systems used for speeches. However, time, place and manner restrictions must be content neutral, meaning the same rules apply to all public gatherings whether or not they are political.

During public gatherings, activists have a constitutional right to photograph or videotape the police, government authorities, and anything else that is plainly visible. This right was confirmed by the Third Circuit Court of Appeals in 2017. The court ruled that two people were legally protected when using their cell phones to record police actions in Philadelphia. Judge Thomas Ambro writes, "Officers are public officials carrying out public functions, and the First Amendment requires them to [tolerate] bystanders recording their actions. This is vital to promote the access that fosters free discussion of governmental actions."[45]

> "Officers are public officials carrying out public functions, and the First Amendment requires them to [tolerate] bystanders recording their actions."[45]
>
> —Thomas Ambro, federal judge

The Supreme Court has further ruled that police may not search your cell phone or camera without a warrant, even if you are under arrest. Furthermore, officials cannot confiscate a smartphone or camera, cannot demand that you delete photographs or videos, and cannot delete your photos or videos on their own.

Obtaining a Permit

Students planning to hold a protest rally might need to obtain a permit. Requirements vary from place to place, and march organizers need to check with the offices of the mayor, county clerk, or police department to determine what is legally permissible. Oftentimes permits are required for marches or gatherings that might disrupt traffic or lead to street closures. In such cases it can take several weeks to obtain a permit. However, there are First Amendment protections in place when protesters wish to react to breaking news events. Courts have ruled that activists may gather to protest without a permit if they are reacting, for example, to a recent police shooting or other current event.

The permitting process is often difficult. Officials sometimes try to restrict routes or impose unrealistic noise levels on sound systems, claiming they are concerned about traffic control or public safety. But permits cannot be denied because an event is unpopular or controversial. The ACLU provides this advice to those who interact with officials during the permitting process: "Know your rights and exercise them in a responsible way, and if you have to interact with law enforcement, school officials, or other authority figures, remember to be polite, calm, and clearly explain how your actions are within your constitutional rights."[46]

The terms *polite*, *calm*, and *clear* can be applied to any situation in which students are exercising their First Amendment rights. Protesting is a sanctified American tradition, but it should not devolve into anger and incoherence. Hardly anyone ever wins an argument just because they shout the loudest. Problems related to civil rights and the environment were solved when activists convinced a majority of Americans that the causes were just and required immediate attention. When students push, school officials and other authorities can be expected to push back. But with more than a half century of court rulings behind them, student activists are legally protected when they peacefully express their views and work toward positive change.

CHAPTER 5

Lessons Learned

> "We're receiving a lot of cruelty [on social media]. . . . The best thing that we can do is push it aside because these people are only giving us hate because they know that it's anonymous. . . . We don't want to fight back because that's just going to diminish our movement."
>
> —Delaney Tarr, joint founder of the Never Again movement
>
> Quoted in Brittney McNamara, "How Parkland Survivors Are Coping with Bullying," *Teen Vogue*, March 9, 2018. www.teenvogue.com.

In 2015 Dillon Eisman was a Malibu, California, middle school student who had an interest in fashion. He never saw himself as a clothing designer, but then he visited the Los Angeles LBGT Center. The homeless kids he met at the center wore drab, donated clothing. As Eisman says, "Often, when people donate the clothes don't fit well and there's no style and honestly, they look horrible."[47] Eisman believed he could help improve the self-esteem of the homeless kids if he could transform their secondhand clothing into fashionable outfits they would be proud to wear. He understood that nice clothing can elevate a person's confidence and mood—and maybe help them land an important job.

Eisman got out his mother's old sewing machine. He taught himself to sew from the wikiHow website and learned to cut patterns and design clothes from YouTube videos. Soon he was buying and remaking (or *upcycling*) inexpensive clothing from thrift stores. In 2015 Eisman brought seven huge bags of upcycled clothing to the LBGT Center. He never met the people who were eligible to receive his clothing; confidentiality issues are in place to help the center protect the identity of its clients. But Eisman's generosity created a very positive public response. Jennifer Dawson,

A California high school student who was distressed to find homeless kids wearing drab, donated clothes began buying, remaking, and distributing inexpensive thrift store clothing. Winning widespread praise and support, he turned his project into a nonprofit organization.

who runs the center, commends Eisman: "Dillon is a brilliant young man who has already made a huge difference in his community as a leader, activist and philanthropist. We're very grateful for all the work he has done."[48] Eisman's vision and hard work also increased his profile at school, where he was elected class president. And an anonymous admirer described Eisman's work to *People* magazine's "Heroes Among Us" section, which featured him in an article. This led to further media coverage on the *NBC Nightly News*.

The public response to the media coverage helped propel Eisman's vision forward. People sent him donations, which Eisman used to found a nonprofit named Sew Swag, created to turn donated clothing into fashionable outfits for homeless teens. And in 2018 Abercrombie & Fitch partnered with Sew Swag to donate new clothing for Eisman's cause.

A Sense of Accomplishment

When Eisman learned to sew, he was not thinking about starting a movement or seeing his face on TV. He just wanted to help other young people. Knowing that he has been able to do that is a good feeling. "When I upcycle clothes for disadvantaged teens, my primary goal is for them to feel confident with who they are through what they wear," Eisman says. "The best thing is knowing I can take something that no one wanted and transform it into something that makes them feel beautiful once they put it on."[49]

While Eisman's story is unique, the arc of his activism is not. Students nationwide have invested their time and energy in a wide array of worthy projects. Some of those projects are small and local; others grow far beyond their local roots. Regardless of the size of their projects, young activists usually describe feeling a sense of accomplishment. New York high school senior Em Odesser is the founder of *Teen Eye Magazine*. She found her journey into the world of activism to be an illuminating experience. After participating in the 2018 March For Our Lives rally, she said:

> "I've come to realize there is a unique kind of power in marching in the streets you're so familiar with, to so radically transform their use from the everyday."[50]
>
> —Em Odesser, founder of *Teen Eye Magazine*

I've come to realize there is a unique kind of power in marching in the streets you're so familiar with, to so radically transform their use from the everyday. It's also a reminder that you're not alone. . . . At protests, there's usually an overwhelming sense that everyone present has each other's backs. For a little bit, time even stops: you forget that your [shoes] are hurting your toes, that you haven't had a sip of water in two hours, that you've in fact never met the people you're linking arms with.[50]

Odesser's activism taught her that young people are capable of mature and intellectual thought. She says she felt pride that she and other high school students were able to spark an intense national dialogue on gun violence, which is usually considered an adult issue. This made her feel a great sense of accomplishment.

Perseverance

While marching for a cause can be an uplifting experience, becoming an activist can also be exhausting and sometimes disappointing. As eighteen-year-old St. Louis, Missouri, high school senior Brian Wingbermuehle explains: "Nearly all of my time is dedicated to politics and school, and I function on a daily basis only due to the . . . caffeine I consume."[51]

Wingbermuehle became an activist in 2016 when he saw that many issues he supported—including a woman's right to make her own decisions about abortion, LGBTQ rights, and protections for undocumented immigrants—were under attack. His activism led him to organize other students, lobby Missouri lawmakers, and drum up support for a US congressional candidate he preferred. Much of the work was time consuming and mundane. At night and on weekends, he worked phone banks, calling hundreds of voters to ask for their support in the coming election. He also canvassed neighborhoods, going door-to-door to promote his candidate. People can be rude and argumentative when they do not agree with a candidate's politics. Wingbermuehle remained poised and polite in the face of hostility.

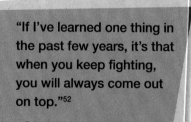

"If I've learned one thing in the past few years, it's that when you keep fighting, you will always come out on top."[52]

—Brian Wingbermuehle, student activist

But activists also need to be persistent as, Wingbermuehle explains: "If I've learned one thing in the past few years, it's that when you keep fighting, you will always come out on top. Even if the interviews fall through or bills and issues you advocated for don't go as you hoped, you've gained experience and you have new contacts in the business. Now you're more prepared for the next battle!"[52]

Dealing with Meanness

One of the biggest battles student activists face is dealing with nasty, negative comments on Twitter, YouTube, Facebook, and other social media sites. Activists who use online platforms to organize can be challenged by well-organized business interests, experienced political operatives, trolls, and cyberbullies. March For Our Lives activist Delaney Tarr uses a technique that can be helpful for any activist dealing with online harassment. She uses humor to reduce bullies to a joke. In one tweet, Tarr posted a

Taking on Trolls

Cyberbullying and harassment have become a fact of life. According to the Pew Research Center, nearly one-third of US teens were cyberbullied in 2017. Teens who take their activism online are likely to experience that sort of ugly behavior. Brittan Heller is an expert in dealing with online bullying and harassment. She is director of technology for the Anti-Defamation League, an organization that tracks anti-Semitism. Heller offers these insights:

> When I became a victim of cyber harassment, I really felt what it was like to be targeted online for my gender and my race and my ethnicity, and more than that I felt how terrifying it can feel to be threatened and how powerless this type of abuse can make you feel, especially when it's coming from anonymous sources.

> First, I'd say you're not alone. Part of the power that the harassers have is they like to make people feel isolated, and sometimes part of the ongoing harm of these kind of crimes is that you feel like there's no meaningful way for you to fight back, there's no way for you to adequately speak out against what's happening to you.

> I would not let the harassment take your voice away. You can talk to family, teachers and friends about what you're experiencing and what you've seen. You can be a support for other people experiencing the same thing, and you can call out people who are trying to incite hate online.

Brittan Heller, "What It's Like to Fight Online Hate," *Taking Note* (blog), *New York Times*, September 16, 2016. https://takingnote.blogs.nytimes.com.

photo of herself smiling broadly and holding a letter she received that was scrawled with obscenities. Tarr's sarcastic caption read: "Love those fans!"[53] The tweet generated hundreds of supportive comments and thousands of likes and shares.

Using humor against aggressors is empowering and is a common way to cope with any type of bullying. But laughing off attackers is only one way activists deal with opponents. MSD sophomore Sarah Chadwick clapped back when cyberbullies mocked her and used the incidents to amplify her movement's message: "I know a lot of people say don't give the trolls attention, don't give them your time. But if the opportunity is there and it's easy, why not? We can spread our word through . . . clap backs. If that's . . . how it goes viral, so be it."[54]

> "I know a lot of people say don't give the trolls attention, don't give them your time. But . . . we can spread our word through . . . clap backs."[54]
>
> —Sarah Chadwick, member of the Never Again movement

Listening to the Other Side

Clapping back can be satisfying. But activists need to listen to what the other side is saying so that they can make logical arguments that might convince opponents to change their view. Canadian activist Seb Paquet believes one of the most common mistakes activists make is ignoring the opinions of those who oppose them. While there is great joy in participating in activist events with like-minded people, Paquet says, "effective activism is about spending time with people who think differently. Listening too much to people who think like they do . . . ends up hindering the effort."[55]

Paquet believes that problems can be solved more effectively if activists make sensible arguments not only to their supporters but also to those who might not

> "Effective activism is about spending time with people who think differently. Listening too much to people who think like they do . . . ends up hindering the effort."[55]
>
> —Seb Paquet, social activist

agree with them. For example, in some parts of the western United States, environmental activists are working with ranchers, who are traditionally seen as opponents. The environmentalists showed that ecological land-management techniques help the ranchers make more money while protecting endangered species. As Paquet explains, the dialogue helps the two sides "see connections, cooperate, and build a network of support with [those] who are pushing other causes."[56]

Balancing Activism and School

Whatever the cause, student activists have to learn to balance their activism with the demands of homework, tests, keeping up grades, and filling out college applications. This can be difficult, as the organizers of the March For Our Lives rally can confirm. While David Hogg was planning a national gun control rally, he was also memorizing his fifty psychology vocabulary words and working on an environmental science project. "That's a lot of stress,"[57] says Hogg.

Student activists need to make sure they do not lose sight of other important parts of their lives. Getting a good night's sleep and keeping up with schoolwork are all part of maintaining a healthy balance.

The size and scope of the March For Our Lives movement meant that Hogg and the other students planning the event were able to rely on parents, teachers, nonprofit groups, and even sympathetic celebrities to take care of the day-to-day planning and work. Most activists do not have that luxury, and this can lead to trouble. As eighteen-year-old North Carolina political activist Mitch Xia explains, "I often find myself falling behind in classes. I don't like that I fall behind for organizing . . . [and] it causes me such anxiety . . . because such weight is assigned to our [grades] and how we do in class."[58]

Student counselors warn that academic pressures coupled with the stress of activism can be unhealthy. Students need to learn to take a break from their activism activities for a few days to regain a sense of balance in their lives. Some suggest set-

Know Your Opponents

Not all causes that students take on have opposition. But some do. When students get involved in a cause that is controversial, there is benefit to talking with those who disagree. Activists who make personal contact with members of the opposition can come to understand the opponent's beliefs, background, opinions, and tactics. One-on-one discussions sometimes lead to compromise. When compromise is not possible, getting to know your opponents can put you in a stronger position to develop how to make your case to the public. The ACLU youth activism manual explains why meeting your opponents is a good idea:

[Opponents] are more likely to fight "fair" if the other side is not a nameless, faceless "enemy." Furthermore, they may be an ally on another issue in the future. Assessing where the opposition is coming from will aid you in determining the best strategy for moving forward with them, whether you negotiate a compromise or battle the issue out in a public forum. If you are going to confront the opposition, spend time considering their strategy. What messages will they use? What research will they point to? What are their available resources? These questions can inform your strategy and action plan.

American Civil Liberties Union of Tennessee, "Stand Up/Speak Up: A Guide for Youth Activists," 2015. www.aclu -tn.org.

ting a sixty- to ninety-minute timer on their phones and focus entirely on schoolwork until the alarm goes off. Taking the time to get enough rest can also help improve concentration and focus on schoolwork. North Carolina student activist Kierra Campbell, who works with the National Association for the Advancement of Colored People, points out the importance of self-care: "[This] involves knowing yourself. . . . You need to recognize when your mind gets tired and when your body reaches its breaking point. When you recognize that, you need to first of all take a step back and stop answering phone calls or answering emails—just rest."[59]

Giving and Receiving

Most student-led campaigns do not require an army of activists and a full-time commitment. Sometimes an organizer working on a small project might go days or weeks without talking to others involved in the endeavor. But whatever the level of commitment, student activists need to remember that life is about more than work. After spending time trying to solve social problems, Campbell likes to go dancing to relieve stress: "It's cheery and just lifted a lot of that weight physically and emotionally off of me. Self-care is . . . [about] activities that uplift your spirit and also really de-stress your mind."[60]

Campbell understands that activism is a learning process that involves more than working a phone bank, marching in the streets, and clapping back on Twitter. Practicing self-care is equally important, along with keeping up with the demands of school. But while the work can be hard, there is a joy in activism. Studies show that those who donate their time to a cause feel more socially connected and experience less loneliness and depression. The spirit is uplifted by making a difference, giving back to the community, and developing new skills. Activists understand that while they are making the world a better place, they are also gaining what Em Odesser calls "a unique kind of power."[61] That sense of pride and accomplishment transcends everyday life and shines a light on what is possible now and what might be attainable in the future.

CHAPTER 6

Perspectives from the Past

"We caught the entire nation by surprise. . . . Before the walkouts, no one cared that substandard schools made it all but impossible for Chicano youths to find strength and pride in their culture, language and history. . . . After the walkouts no one could deny that . . . with better education, the Chicano community could control its own destiny."

—David Sanchez, social activist and founder of the Brown Berets

Quoted in Louis Sahagun, "East L.A., 1968: 'Walkout!' The Day High School Students Helped Ignite the Chicano Power Movement," *Los Angeles Times*, March 1, 2018. www.latimes.com.

The action had been planned for months, and the students were warned not to participate. Despite threats of punishment from teachers and authorities, thousands of student activists from high schools, middle schools, and even elementary schools walked out of their classrooms and gathered in the streets. The students hoisted picket signs and organized themselves into a line of marchers. Raising their voices in song, the young activists headed toward city hall to meet with politicians and air their grievances. The eyes of the world were focused on the activists as dozens of reporters and photographers covered the action.

The year was 1963. On May 2 of that year, thousands of African American students marched in the streets of Birmingham, Alabama. The student walkout, which lasted more than a week, launched what was later referred to as the Children's Crusade. And the actions taken by these young protesters have provided numerous historical lessons to generations of student activists who followed.

At the time of the Children's Crusade, Birmingham was one of the most repressive cities in the country. Black people were segregated in schools, parks, movie theaters, restaurants, and other public places. Civil rights leader Martin Luther King Jr. and other adult members of the civil rights movement had tried—and failed—to integrate Birmingham. As their efforts faltered, civil rights organizer James Bevel came up with another idea. He began recruiting boys who were athletes and girls who were student leaders. These students enlisted others until several thousand were willing to participate. Bevel and other civil rights leaders trained the students in nonviolent protest techniques, and the students were required to sign a pledge of nonviolence.

The protesters followed the techniques they had learned, marching peacefully through downtown Birmingham. They were met with brutal violence. The Birmingham commissioner of public safety, Eugene "Bull" Connor, ordered fire hoses to be turned on the students. As news cameras rolled, water pressure strong enough to rip bark from trees pushed student protesters over cars and blasted them down city streets. Police brought out attack dogs and turned them on the student marchers as photographers recorded the scene. The photos, which showed the bravery and determination of the black students, were splashed across the front pages of newspapers throughout the world. President John F. Kennedy said he was sickened by the images.

On the first day of the walkout, more than six hundred students were arrested. As the crusade continued, hundreds more were jailed, but fresh recruits stood ready to replace them. When the city jails were full, the activists were imprisoned in a makeshift stockade at the local fairgrounds. The sight of children being brutalized and imprisoned brought outside pressure on city leaders to end the protests. On May 10 Birmingham city officials began negotiations with King and other civil rights leaders to lay out a plan to integrate the city. Connor was removed from his position. The Children's Crusade had succeeded.

One of the protesters was Gwen Gamble. She was fifteen at the time. In 2013, on the fiftieth anniversary of the demonstration,

A police dog attacks a seventeen-year-old student protester in May 1963 in Birmingham, Alabama. Students played a big role in civil rights movement protests, including this walkout by thousands of African American students.

Gamble credited the student action for sparking a wider movement to integrate the South—and for eventually helping elect the nation's first black president. She said, "Had it not been for those children going out in the streets of Birmingham making a difference, going to jail, protesting, I really don't believe what we have today would be possible. I definitely say there would not be a Barack Obama."[62]

Taking Action to Improve Schools

As student activists make headlines today protesting gun violence, immigration issues, and racism, they can take inspiration from successful 1960s civil rights actions. While the movement is often remembered for its adult leaders such as King, Fannie Lou Hamer, Malcolm X, and others, students were performing some of the most difficult work. They were leading sit-ins, marching in demonstrations, and holding voter registration drives. Although many of the students were in college, the movement also attracted younger participants who led their own activist projects.

> "Had it not been for those children going out in the streets of Birmingham making a difference, going to jail, protesting, I really don't believe what we have today would be possible."[62]
>
> —Gwen Gamble, participant in the 1963 Children's Crusade

In the wake of the Birmingham march, students in Chicago and New York City also decided to act. Fed up with conditions in their schools, they took to the streets. In Chicago more than 250,000 walked out of classes on October 22, 1963, to protest city schools that were segregated, overcrowded, and underfunded. The students marched to the city's Board of Education building, where they planned to hand a list of demands to the superintendent. Police prevented the students from entering the building.

The Chicago walkout failed to convince politicians to institute changes. But the action inspired a February 1964 protest in New York City that involved 460,000 African American and Puerto Rican high school kids who faced the same problems as students in Chicago. After the one-day walkout, New York officials promised to improve the quality of education and ease overcrowding in schools attended by nonwhite students.

Having a Voice

Student protests in Birmingham, Chicago, and New York City provided a model for similar walkouts a few years later in Los Angeles. In 1968 about ten thousand students from five East Los Angeles high schools protested conditions in their schools. Their list of grievances included overcrowding, high dropout rates, run-down classrooms, outdated textbooks, racist teachers, lack of college prep courses, and a curriculum that ignored Mexican American history. Most of the student protesters were of Mexican descent. They were joined by African American students from a nearby school. The walkout, which they called a blowout, lasted fifteen days.

While the blowouts surprised teachers and authorities, they were an outgrowth of student activism that had been blossoming for years. In 1963, when there was little information available to students who wished to launch protests, a Malibu summer camp called Camp Hess Kramer began hosting motivational programs for outstanding Hispanic students. By 1967 the program was bringing together groups of students who spent their days brainstorming ways to fix their neglected schools and depressed neighborhoods. Today the Camp Hess Kramer program would be called intersectional; students from different racial, religious, and economic backgrounds crossed paths in the program. Many Hispanic students who attended the camp enhanced their activism skills at the Social Action Training Center at the Los An-

Not Supported by the Public

Student activists can learn strategies and skills from past protest movements. But they should understand that no matter how righteous the perceived cause, mass demonstrations are rarely popular with the general public. For example, in 1963 Americans widely opposed the tactics used in the Children's Crusade. A Gallup poll taken just weeks after the protests ended in Birmingham asked if the mass demonstrations were more likely to help or hurt the cause for racial equality. Around two-thirds of Americans said the demonstrations would hurt the cause. Fewer than 23 percent had a favorable view of the protest. When broken down by race, the numbers are starker; 85 percent of white people said the actions would hurt African Americans.

While the sit-ins, marches, and walkouts of the past are viewed today with historical reverence, they were very controversial at the time. But like today's activists, those who marched in the 1960s were not concerned about how they might be judged in the future. As civil rights activist Joyce Ladner explains: "[We] did it for ourselves. We weren't aware of history at that time, or that one day it would go down in history, because these events were in the moment. We didn't have time to focus on [the] long-term."

Quoted in Elahe Izadi, "Black Lives Matter and America's Long History of Resisting Civil Rights Protesters," *Washington Post*, April 19, 2016. www.washingtonpost.com.

geles Church of the Epiphany. As Vickie Castro, who attended both centers, later commented: "We were all products of Camp Kramer and Church of the Epiphany and, therefore, aspired to remake society."[63]

One of the students who participated in these programs, seventeen-year-old David Sanchez, opened the La Piranya coffee shop, which became headquarters for the blowout campaign. Long before social media, the students spread word of the planned blowouts through underground newspapers, flyers, and community events at the coffee shop. Students from the University of California–Los Angeles and other local colleges were brought in to serve as mentors.

While the blowouts did not immediately improve East Los Angeles schools, the action had long-lasting consequences, as participant Moctesuma Esparza explains: "The No. 1 thing that the walkouts achieved is that it gave our own community a voice—that we didn't have to rely on what other people thought we should be doing or who we should be."[64]

> "The No. 1 thing that the walkouts achieved is that it gave our own community a voice—that we didn't have to rely on what other people thought we should be doing or who we should be."[64]
>
> —Moctesuma Esparza, community activist

The Antiwar Movement

While some worked at the local level to demand better schools, other students in the 1960s took part in the antiwar movement. The movement began to grow in 1965 after the United States became deeply involved in fighting Communist soldiers in Vietnam. In this era before the all-volunteer army, around 25 percent of the half-million Americans in Vietnam were drafted. They were required by law to join the military. College students could defer being drafted. But high school students who did not plan to attend college faced the draft as soon as they graduated. The draft was unpopular, and many Americans opposed the war on moral grounds. Additionally, by 1967 the war was not going well for the United States, and many came to believe the conflict was unwinnable. This combination of factors led to the formation of the largest antiwar movement in American history.

The first major antiwar protests took place in 1967, and high school students were involved. An April protest in New York City attracted nearly half a million people, including a large percentage of high school and college students. The demonstration was organized by the Spring Mobilization Committee to End the War in Vietnam, commonly referred to as the Mobe. James Bevel, who had organized the Children's Crusade in 1963, was chair of the Mobe. In a 1985 interview, Bevel explained why he encouraged high school students to join the antiwar movement: "Guys [as young as] seventeen were in Vietnam and our thinking was that if a young person could go to Vietnam and engage in a war, then the person certainly the same age and younger could engage in a non-violent war [protest] that didn't violate the constitution."[65]

Like other mass protests at the time, the antiwar movement was not popular; around 70 percent of Americans opposed dem-

Demonstrators in Washington, DC, take part in a May 1972 sit-in to protest US involvement in the Vietnam War. High school and college students were at the forefront of the antiwar movement.

Coffee Shop Activists

The La Piranya coffee shop became the headquarters for the 1968 East Los Angeles high school blowouts. The coffee shop was the brainchild of seventeen-year-old David Sanchez, who wrote a successful grant proposal to the Southern California Council of Churches in 1967. The grant provided funds for the coffee shop, which became a teen hangout and home to several student political groups, including the Young Chicanos for Community Action and the United Mexican American Students. The coffee shop was a hub of activity, where protesters wrote articles for underground newspapers and designed flyers that were handed out in the neighborhood.

Sanchez even used fashion to spread the message of Chicano activism at his after-school job supervising an elementary school playground. He began wearing a stylish, flat brown cap, which inspired the children to call him Brown Beret. Sanchez taught the kids about the Chicano movement. In 1970 he founded the Brown Berets organization, which coordinated student protests in Arizona, Texas, New Mexico, Chicago, and elsewhere. The Brown Berets group, while small, is still active today.

onstrating against the war, while one-third believed protesting should be illegal. Against this backdrop, teenagers who chose to protest were often labeled as revolutionaries, agitators, and Communists. And like the students in Birmingham, many faced violence from authorities wielding billy clubs, attack dogs, and tear gas.

As the war continued, anger and frustration increased, and violence escalated on both sides. When President Richard Nixon announced an expansion of the war in April 1970, student protests broke out across the country. On May 4 National Guard troops shot and killed four students and wounded nine others at Kent State University in Ohio. Four days later a massive school walkout was held to protest the shootings. Four million students at 450 junior high schools, high schools, colleges, and universities across the country took part. Students gathered in major cities to march, listen to speeches, and sing songs. Over 100,000 protested in New York City; another 150,000 turned out in San Francisco. While the protests were mostly peaceful, some became violent. That happened in Washington, DC, where student protesters broke windows, slashed tires, and overturned cars. At one point Nixon was evacuated from the White House because of concerns for his safety.

Despite the efforts of the antiwar movement the Vietnam War dragged on until 1975. What is more, the anger, violence, and rebelliousness of the era left many Americans with a lasting negative opinion of student protest movements. But for some of the participants, the antiwar movement was life changing. Maurice Isserman was sixteen years old when he attended the 1967 Mobe action in New York City. Fifty years later Isserman recalled the positive aspects of the movement: "When antiwar protesters gathered, I came to feel, we did so not just to express ourselves as dissenters, which is to say, angry outsiders, but in the best interests and representing the best instincts of the nation."[66]

Today and Tomorrow

Today students in movements as diverse as Black Lives Matter, United We Dream, and Never Again continue to generate controversy and praise as they oppose entrenched government policies. But in the starkly different environment of the twenty-first century, social media is allowing students to build national movements in a matter of days and weeks, rather than years. While the technology of activism has changed, the tactics remain the same. Students gather at coffee shops, write articles, print flyers, and encourage others to speak out. They work with established organizations and plan national demonstrations.

If the history of student protest proves anything, modern activists are not wasting their time when they march, boycott, and engage in walkouts. Today, tomorrow, and in the years to come, student activists will shift and shape society, driven by ideals and following tactics that were used by their parents and grandparents who protested injustice in the past.

SOURCE NOTES

INTRODUCTION: CREATING CHANGE

1. Quoted in Jenny Jarvie, "Sensing Their Moment, Florida Students Balance School and Activism Planning the March For Our Lives," *Los Angeles Times*, March 22, 2018. www.latimes.com.
2. Quoted in Savonne Anderson, "8 Ways to Meaningfully Support Social Justice Movements," Mashable, March 26, 2016. https://mashable.com.
3. Quoted in Mark Keierleber, "17 Minutes of History: Wednesday's Walkout Part of Long Tradition of Students Speaking Out, from *Tinker v. Des Moines* to Black Lives Matter," 74, March 13, 2018. www.the74million.org.
4. Quoted in Dan Berrett, "Teaching Newsletter: Just Maybe Student Activists Aren't So Closed-Minded," *Chronicle of Higher Education*, November 16, 2017. www.chronicle.com.
5. Quoted in Elizabeth Marie Himchak, "Girl Scout Honored by President for Volunteerism," *San Diego Union-Tribune*, April 18, 2018. www.sandiegouniontribune.com.

CHAPTER ONE: CAN STUDENTS MAKE A DIFFERENCE?

6. Marley Dias, *Marley Dias Gets It Done: And So Can You!* New York: Scholastic, 2018, pp. 29–30.
7. Dias, *Marley Dias Gets It Done*, p. 31.
8. Dias, *Marley Dias Gets It Done*, p. 56.
9. Quoted in Alison Thoet, "13-Year-Old Founder of #1000BlackGirlBooks Shares Some of Her Favorite Reads," *PBS NewsHour*, February 16, 2018. www.pbs.org.
10. Quoted in Ecology Center, "Featured Thought Leader: Jackson Hinkle," January 17, 2018. www.theecologycenter.org.
11. Jackson Hinkle, "Plastic Free CUSD," *Triton Times* (San Clemente High School student newspaper), January 17, 2018. https://tritontimes.com.
12. Quoted in The Ecology Center, "Featured Thought Leader."
13. Quoted in David Moberg, "Obama's Community Roots," *Nation*, April 3, 2007. www.thenation.com.
14. Xiuhtezcatl Martinez, *We Rise*. El Segundo, CA: Rodale, 2017, p. 19.
15. Quoted in Martinez, *We Rise*, p. 22.

16. Martinez, *We Rise*, p. 22.
17. Martinez, *We Rise*, p. 24.

CHAPTER TWO: TURNING TRAGEDY INTO ACTION

18. Garance Franke-Ruta, "Aurora and the Template of Our Grief," *Atlantic*, July 20, 2012. www.theatlantic.com.
19. Quoted in Jared Keller, "Dissecting America's Muted Response to Mass Shootings," *Pacific Standard*, February 15, 2018. https://psmag.com.
20. Quoted in CNN, "Florida Student Emma Gonzalez to Lawmakers and Gun Advocates: 'We Call BS,'" February 17, 2018. www.cnn.com.
21. Lisa Miller, "War Room," *New York*, March 2, 2018, http://nymag.com.
22. Quoted in Beth Greenfield, "March For Our Lives and Gay Activism: 'They're Definitely Linked for Me,' says Emma González," Yahoo! News, March 25, 2018. www.yahoo.com.
23. Quoted in Matt Pearce, "When It Comes to Guns, Parkland Shooting Survivors Aren't Here to Play Nice," *Los Angeles Times*, February 23, 2018. www.latimes.com.
24. Quoted in Jonah Engel Bromwich, "How Parkland Students Got So Good at Social Media," *New York Times*, March 7, 2018. www.nytimes.com.
25. Quoted in Jake Nevins, "Late-Night Hosts on Trump's Parkland Comments: 'We Already Know How You React to Combat,'" *Guardian* (Manchester), February 27, 2018. www.theguardian.com.
26. Quoted in Miller, "War Room."
27. March For Our Lives, "Toolkit," 2018. https://everytown.org/documents/2018/03/march-for-our-lives-toolkit.pdf.
28. Barack Obama's Twitter page, February 22, 2018. https://twitter.com.
29. Quoted in David Adams and Antonio Cucho, "How the NRA Made Florida the 'Gunshine' State," Univision News, February 24, 2018. www.univision.com.
30. Quoted in AJ Willingham, "Slacktivism Is Over. The #NeverAgain Movement Is About What's Next," CNN, March 26, 2018. www.cnn.com.

CHAPTER THREE: TAKING ACTION

31. Dias, *Marley Dias Gets It Done*, p. 98.
32. Stephen R. Covey, *The 7 Habits of Highly Effective People*. New York: Simon & Schuster, 1989, p. 41.

33. American Civil Liberties Union of Tennessee, "Stand Up/Speak Up: A Guide for Youth Activists," 2015. www.aclu-tn.org.
34. Quoted in Allison Pohle, "How a Group of Boston Teenagers Organized a Massive District-Wide Protest," *Boston Globe*, March 11, 2016. www.boston.com.
35. American Civil Liberties Union of Tennessee, "Stand Up/Speak Up."
36. Dias, *Marley Dias Gets It Done*, p. 107.
37. Quoted in Mariah Balingit, "'This Is a Marathon': Delaney Tarr's Quest for Common-Sense Gun Laws," *Washington Post*, February 21, 2018. www.washingtonpost.com.
38. Dias, *Marley Dias Gets It Done*, p. 109.
39. Dias, *Marley Dias Gets It Done*, p. 98.

CHAPTER FOUR: KNOW YOUR RIGHTS

40. Abe Fortas, *Tinker v. Des Moines Independent Community School Dist.*, 393 U.S. 503 (1969).
41. Fortas, *Tinker v. Des Moines Independent Community School Dist.*
42. Stephen Reinhardt et al., *Harper v. Poway Unified School District: 20*, No. 04-57037 (2006). https://caselaw.findlaw.com.
43. Quoted in Bob Keeler, "Pennridge Students Received Detention for Participating in National School Walkout," *Lansdale (PA) Reporter*, March 15, 2018. www.thereporteronline.com.
44. Quoted in Judy Woodruff, "Schools Are Watching Students' Social Media, Raising Questions About Free Speech," *PBS NewsHour*, June 20, 2017. www.pbs.org.
45. Quoted in Matt Ford, "A Major Victory for the Right to Record Police," *Atlantic*, July 7, 2017. www.theatlantic.com.
46. American Civil Liberties Union of Tennessee, "Stand Up/Speak Up."

CHAPTER FIVE: LESSONS LEARNED

47. Quoted in Susan Young, "California High Schooler Helps Clothe Homeless Teens with His Own Designs," *People*, March 16, 2017. https://people.com.
48. Quoted in Young, "California High Schooler Helps Clothe Homeless Teens with His Own Designs."
49. Quoted in Young, "California High Schooler Helps Clothe Homeless Teens with His Own Designs."
50. Em Odesser, "The Lessons a Teen Activist Wants You to Learn from the March For Our Lives," *W*, March 25, 2018. www.wmagazine.com.
51. Brian Wingbermuehle, "7 Tips to Balancing Activism and School Work," *Teen Vogue*, April 18, 2018. www.teenvogue.com.

52. Wingbermuehle, "7 Tips to Balancing Activism and School Work."
53. Quoted in Christianna Silva, "Parkland Survivor Delaney Tarr Is Receiving Hate Mail," *Teen Vogue*, March 7, 2018. www.teenvogue .com.
54. Quoted in Brittney McNamara, "How Parkland Survivors Are Coping with Bullying," *Teen Vogue*, March 9, 2018. www.teenvogue .com.
55. Seb Paquet, "What Are Some Common Mistakes That Activists Make?," Quora, February 25, 2013. www.quora.com.
56. Paquet, "What Are Some Common Mistakes That Activists Make?"
57. Quoted in Jarvie, "Sensing Their Moment, Florida Students Balance School and Activism Planning the March For Our Lives."
58. Quoted in Victoria Mirian, "Tipping the Balance: Activism and Academics Compete for Student's Attention," *Daily Tar Heel* (University of North Carolina–Chapel Hill student newspaper), April 25, 2016. www.dailytarheel.com.
59. Quoted in Mirian, "Tipping the Balance."
60. Quoted in Mirian, "Tipping the Balance."
61. Odesser, "The Lessons a Teen Activist Wants You to Learn from the March For Our Lives."

CHAPTER SIX: PERSPECTIVES FROM THE PAST

62. Quoted in Lottie L. Joiner, "How the Children of Birmingham Changed the Civil Rights Movement," *Daily Beast*, May 2, 2013. www.thedailybeast.com.
63. Quoted in Louis Sahagun, "East L.A., 1968: 'Walkout!' The Day High School Students Helped Ignite the Chicano Power Movement," *Los Angeles Times*, March 1, 2018. www.latimes.com.
64. Quoted in Louis Sahagun, "They Faced 66 Years in Prison. The 'Eastside 13' and How They Helped Plan the East L.A. Walkouts," *Los Angeles Times*, March 8, 2018. www.latimes.com.
65. Quoted in Washington University Digital Library, "Eyes on the Prize: Interviews," November 13, 1985. http://digital.wustl.edu.
66. Maurice Isserman, "My First Antiwar Protest," *New York Times*, April 14, 2017. www.nytimes.com.

RESOURCES FOR STUDENT ACTIVISTS

Advice on Leading Change from Experienced Youth Activists and Allies

www.youthinfront.org

Youth in Front, a community-created online learning resource for student activists, developed this resource. Through a mix of YouTube videos and other types of presentations, teen and adult activists address questions such as: Will I get in trouble? How do I organize a protest? How do I get adults on my side? How does a march become a movement?

March For Our Lives Toolkit

https://everytown.org/documents/2018/03/march-for-our-lives-toolkit.pdf

This detailed how-to guide was created to assist students planning March For Our Lives events nationwide. Other teen activists may find this guide useful for organizing and publicizing events of various types.

Stand Up/Speak Up: A Guide for Youth Activists

www.aclu-tn.org/wp-content/uploads/2016/05/Youth-Activism-Manual-2015.pdf

Created by the Tennessee chapter of the ACLU, this online step-by-step handbook explains how students can create their own social movements by developing action plans, building coalitions, and working with media.

WalkWoke

www.walkwoke.com

This free, downloadable app can be a valuable tool for creating artwork and printable posters from over one thousand customizable templates created by artists. Posters cover dozens of activist causes.

Classroom Walkouts and School Protests

www.freedomforuminstitute.org/first-amendment-center/primers/18655-2

This offering from the Freedom Forum Institute, the education and outreach partner of the nonpartisan Freedom Forum (whose focus is First Amendment freedoms), discusses student rights and responsibilities in connection with classroom walkouts and school protests. A useful FAQ section provides additional information on many common concerns.

Students' Rights: Speech, Walkouts, and Other Protests

www.aclu.org/issues/free-speech/student-speech-and-privacy/students-rights-speech-walkouts-and-other-protests

This site, created by the ACLU, provides details on the Constitutional rights of young people in connection with free speech, protests, and walkouts. There is also a link to the ACLU Summer Advocacy Institute for high school juniors and seniors.

• •

Volunteen Nation

www.volunteennation.org

The organization is run by middle school, high school, and college students from across the country. The organization's website includes a searchable database for youth volunteer opportunities. Members also assist with service projects, offer inspiration and guidance through their blogs, and share information about community-based service resources.

• •

Marley Dias, *Marley Dias Gets It Done: And So Can You!* New York: Scholastic, 2018.

Laurie Collier Hillstrom, *Black Lives Matter: From a Moment to a Movement*. Santa Barbara, CA: Greenwood, 2018.

David Hogg and Lauren Hogg, *#NeverAgain: A New Generation Draws the Line*. New York: Random House, 2018.

Xiuhtezcatl Martinez, *We Rise*. El Segundo, CA: Rodale, 2017.

Scott Myers-Lipton, *CHANGE! A Student Guide to Social Activism*. New York: Routledge, 2017.

Peggy J. Parks, *The Black Lives Matter Movement*. San Diego, CA: ReferencePoint Press, 2018.

KaeLyn Rich, *Girls Resist! A Guide to Activism, Leadership, and Starting a Revolution*. Philadelphia: Quirk, 2018.

American Civil Liberties Union (ACLU)

www.aclu.org

The ACLU defends individual rights and liberties guaranteed by the Constitution and other laws. The organization's website features articles on student rights, free speech, racial justice, and more. The ACLU's Summer Advocacy Institute for high school students features classroom sessions, lectures, and debates run by lawyers, lobbyists, community activists, and other experts.

Black Lives Matter

https://blacklivesmatter.com

Black Lives Matter was founded by three women in 2014 as a response to violence perpetrated against African Americans. The group organizes demonstrations and other events and works to advance legislation to improve the lives of black Americans.

Democracy Matters

www.democracymatters.org

This nonpartisan student organization is working to guide the next generation of leaders to strengthen the democratic institutions of the United States. Students in the group work to organize pro-democracy actions and projects centered on issues such as the environment, education, health care, civil rights, and foreign policy.

Earth Guardians

www.earthguardians.org

This worldwide environmental association, led by the young indigenous activist Xiuhtezcatl Martinez, works to slow climate change. The website provides comprehensive information about organizing, training, and taking action that can be of use to any student activist working on local or global issues.

March For Our Lives

https://marchforourlives.com

March For Our Lives is a gun control organization founded by students at Marjory Stoneman Douglas High School in Parkland, Florida, after a gunman killed seventeen students and staff members there in 2018. The website updates visitors about the latest group events, including school walkouts, mass demonstrations, and national voter registration actions.

CNN, "Florida Student Emma Gonzalez to Lawmakers and Gun Advocates: 'We Call BS,'" February 17, 2018.

Maggie McGrath, "From Activist to Author: How 12-Year-Old Marley Dias Is Changing the Face of Children's Literature," *Forbes*, June 13, 2017.

Brittney McNamara, "How Parkland Survivors Are Coping with Bullying," *Teen Vogue*, March 9, 2018.

Lisa Miller, "War Room," *New York*, March 2, 2018.

Matt Pearce, "When It Comes to Guns, Parkland Shooting Survivors Aren't Here to Play Nice," *Los Angeles Times*, February 23, 2018.

Alison Thoet, "13-Year-Old Founder of #1000BlackGirlBooks Shares Some of Her Favorite Reads," *PBS NewsHour*, February 16, 2018.

INDEX